T0194931

Ode to Grace
A Moment of Prayer

Seeking God? Join Him in Prayer—
Any Day, Any Time with Everyday
Prayers for Everyday Moments

Kathleen Walker Van Karnes

WESTBOW
PRESS®
A DIVISION OF THOMAS NELSON
& ZONDERVAN

WestBow Press books may be ordered through booksellers or by contacting:

WestBow Press
A Division of Thomas Nelson & Zondervan
1663 Liberty Drive
Bloomington, IN 47403
www.westbowpress.com
1 (866) 928-1240

ISBN: 978-1-9736-1047-2 (sc)
ISBN: 978-1-9736-1048-9 (hc)
ISBN: 978-1-9736-1046-5 (e)

Library of Congress Control Number: 2017918950

Print information available on the last page.

WestBow Press rev. date: 01/25/2018

Contents

Chapter 3: Prayers for Renewal

Chapter 4: Prayers for Strength

Chapter 5: Prayers for Peace

Chapter 6: Prayers for Reconciliation

Chapter 7: Prayers for Contemplation

Chapter 8: Prayers for Involvement

Chapter 9: Seasonal Prayers

Chapter 10: Holiday Prayers

Chapter 11: Choir Prayers

Dedication

For my daughter Elisabeth, whose loving encouragement as I composed these prayers meant everything to me. I am doubly blessed to have her join me in prayer every day;

For my husband Robert and our entire family, who sustain and uplift me;

For my other family, the choir at San Marino Community Church. Their amazing voices, loving fellowship and generosity of spirit continue to enrich my life;

And finally, to all who recite these prayers aloud, in communion with our Lord, I hope they enrich your life as they have mine.

My prayer for you, dear child of God, is that as you read this little book, one prayer at a time, the Lord will speak to you and bless you as He has blessed me.

Foreword

As I dragged my suitcase up the stairs, returning home from another long and tiring business trip, I tripped on the top step and fell. I sank into a chair to examine my twisted and rapidly swelling ankle, and I sighed as deeply as I had ever sighed in my life. Hard work and the demands of being a new mother at a somewhat advanced age were wearing me out. I knew that decisions needed to be made about the future and that those decisions needed to be arrived at with God's grace and guidance. But the truth was, my work as a television writer and producer had kept me so busy that quiet moments for prayer came rarely, and when I found them, my head was so full of details that it was getting harder to find the words I thought I should say. And now, sitting with my sprained ankle propped up on a pillow, too tired to hobble back downstairs for an ice pack, it occurred to me that this was the first chance I'd had in a long time to sit down and feel much of anything at all.

In that moment, I discovered that although God certainly didn't sprain my ankle, He was about to use it to get my attention. After completing more than two hundred television episodes about God's unconditional love for us and His desire to participate in every aspect of our lives, I thought I had written everything I could think of about prayer. But there was still more to learn.

My almost-three-year-old Isabel toddled up to me and said, "What happened, Mama?"

Another sigh. "I hurt my foot."

Isabel looked up and said, "I can make it better, Mama. I am going to pray for your foot." She put her hands on my ankle and closed her eyes and spoke the simplest prayer in the world. She spoke the only prayer she knew in the absolute confidence that the Alpha and Omega, the Creator of the universe, the Great Physician, and the Great I Am would hear her, and this was her prayer: "God is great, God is good, and we thank Him for this food. Amen."

I don't know if it was my laughter or my tears that lessened my pain that day, but the lesson she taught me has lasted for years, even as our now-teen-aged Isabel prepares—not surprisingly—to study medicine.

Isabel understood as a child what so many of us often forget as adults—that prayer is not about the "right words" or "the right time" or "the right way." It's about finding whatever is in our hearts that is true—gratitude, love, hope, pain, anger, fear, wonder, and desire— expressing it in the only way we know how, and trusting that God will fill in the blanks.

The Bible says, "For if there be first a willing mind, it is accepted according to that which a person has, not according to what he doesn't have" (2 Cor. 8:12). Now, tiny Isabel didn't know how to read the Bible, but she knew one prayer and recognized that it needed to be said. Granted, it sounded like she was planning to have my foot for dinner, but she trusted God to know what her heart was trying to say. She took whatever she had to work with and laid it at the altar because "from the abundance of the heart, the mouth speaks" (Luke 6:45).

Not long after that little prayer, my family and I began attending San Marino Community Church. My husband, Jon Andersen, and I made the decision to stop working for a while and to devote time to raising our children and to recovering from nearly ten demanding years as the producers of the top ten television drama *Touched by an Angel*.

As gratifying as it had been to share our faith with millions every Sunday night on CBS, Jon and I were now ready to settle down and worship together on Sunday mornings in a neighborhood church with great teaching, great music, and great friends. We found all of that and more at San Marino Community Church, and that is where we came to love and admire Kathy Van Karnes.

Kathy's faithfulness, like that of so many at our beloved church, is a source of encouragement, optimism, and yes, joy to our family. Whether she leads us as a deacon and elder of the congregation, blesses us as chaplain and singer in our outstanding choir, or simply greets us in the courtyard after the service as our friend, her prayer work is an unfailing example of faith in action. Her dedication to lift up her friends and her church in fellowship and in prayer reminds me every Sunday of the powerful peace and the peaceful power of a prayer simply offered from the heart.

Ode to Grace offers us clear, consistent, and authentic language, which reminds us that when we pray in truth, prayer is the easiest language in the world to speak. Kathy's prayers are surely more specific and eloquent than my Isabel's table grace for an ailing ankle, but in every one of Kathy's prayers there can be found the same simple but great lesson: Whatever words of love we know, whatever prayers we can pray, whether out loud or in the quiet corners of our hearts, we can come boldly before the throne of God and speak those words with the confidence that our loving God has been waiting to hear them. And then, whatever His answer, the peace of God, which passes all understanding, will be ours in Christ Jesus.

Martha Williamson

Los Angeles, California 2018

Preface

Sometimes I ponder how I came to write this modest volume. For me, prayer has always been something private, presenting a time for contemplation about and communing with the Lord—just the two of us. As far back as I can remember, I have relied on prayer for guidance, strength, and inspiration. This was especially true at bedtime, because for me, nightly prayers before sleep were among the most meaningful and enriching moments of daily life.

This nighttime custom grew to include not only prayers for those in need but also to urge positive resolutions to situations that involved human peril. At some point, the desire to pray wouldn't keep until bedtime, so I began my day by reciting "The Lord's Prayer." I then continued with thanksgiving for all the blessings I had been given, asked the Lord to continue to bless and protect my family and friends, and offered special petitions for those who needed them. I would close my prayer time by asking the Lord to lead me into the day and to make my actions pleasing to Him.

For years, my Bible studies class at San Marino Community Church ended its weekly study sessions with a prayer or two. Then in 2004, I was invited to join a small group at the church to study *The Purpose Driven Life*—the best-selling devotional book by evangelical Christian pastor Rick Warren. Nine women turned out for the first meeting. Near the end, each was invited to say a little prayer.

Oh my goodness, I thought, *I have never prayed aloud.* I was moved by the others' contributions and how at ease they seemed while praying aloud. Each added a little something different, which enriched the overall experience and helped bond our little group. We've been together ever since.

Over time, friendships developed and deepened as we delved into books about a wide range of biblical subjects. Our faith and understanding grew, underscoring the awareness of God's presence and intentions in our lives.

We took prayer requests from each other and from friends and family outside the group. We shared our struggles and joys, continuing to close our meetings with prayers and petitions. I began to feel comfortable praying aloud in this small, tight-knit group.

My husband, Robert, and I sing in our church choir. At Robert's first meeting after being elected choir president, he cornered me with a question. "Will you close us in prayer at the end of the meeting?"

I panicked. Was he kidding? I gazed at the fifty or so faces in the room. I thought, *How can I do that? What should I say? How do I do this? I'm not prepared.*

I'm fully aware of the irony in what happened next. I closed my eyes and prayed silently but fiercely to the Lord to help me find the words.

When the time came, I asked everyone to stand and to join me in prayer. I couldn't possibly tell you what I said that night. I merely trusted that God would provide the words. Apparently, He did.

Before long, I was invited to serve as choir chaplain. Again, I doubted myself. I thought, *Oh, Lord, You are pulling me in a direction I've never been in before.* Yet somehow, I felt certain God would lead me.

I began to write weekly prayers and was surprised and delighted to discover that there was so much to pray about. Situations and needs could be so different, and more than ever, I came to understand that most people's paths in life are neither smooth nor obvious.

Life is such a grab bag of powerful emotions and character-shaping experiences—love, joy, gratitude, pain, loss, sorrow, struggle, anger, rage, and grief—you name it. What could I bring to those in need at such quiet moments of reflection?

I soon surmised that many people didn't take time to pray. So what kind of bite-sized spiritual nourishments could I offer? Moreover, what words would be sufficiently meaningful to help carry them through the following week? How could I encourage fellow congregants to commune with our magnificent triune God, all day long, as they went about their lives? This became my weekly goal, and I opened myself to what God wanted me to share.

My wonderful daughter, Elisabeth, listened each week to the prayers I had prepared for choir practice. As these contemplations grew to encompass other areas and events, she became my sounding board and cheerleader.

"Mother, you need to put these prayers into a book," she finally told me. "People would welcome it to help them along life's path."

My choir family lovingly validated my work, welcoming the prayer time during which they connected with the Lord and each other. I was serving the Lord but was still amazed how unexpectedly He stepped in front of me to offer direction. He said, *Turn left. I want to use you in a new way.*

People thanked me for my prayers and often asked for copies of them. I was especially touched when someone would say that a particular prayer expressed precisely how he or she felt or what that person had needed to hear. My prayers spoke to them, which I found thrilling. I was humbled and grateful beyond words to serve our Lord in this way. I was making a difference.

—Kathy Van Karnes

Los Angeles, California

1

Everyday Prayers

There are times in the day when you can stop and say a simple little prayer. In this way, you ground yourself and share a few moments with our Lord in prayer. It can brighten your day!

A Minute a Day

Loving God,
For each minute of every day,
may we give thanks to You by spending
a minute in communion with You.
It's a little moment when we can reconnect with the pure
beauty of Your love and dwell in the
presence of Your grace, quietly resting there
at peace with You.

Amen.

A Love So Engrossing

Heavenly Father,

You have given us a love so engrossing, full,
and complete.
We feel Your love, and it warms us to our very
cores.
How safe we feel in Your presence, wrapped
in Your love.
We thank You for this gift.
But there is more.
Filled with this love, we are instructed to pour this love
on others, expansively and without limit, just as You have
given it to us.
Love one another—without exclusion.
What a tall and challenging task it is to love all.
Help us, Lord, to pour out our love.
Stretch us beyond what we think we can do.
We know You are right beside us, encouraging us,
and smiling at us as we forge on.
We can make a difference—each and every one of us.

Amen.

Concerns for Our World

Heavenly Father,

We have deep concerns for our world at this time—
our world of global unrest and conflict and a flood of people
fleeing violence.
They are tired, hungry, and scared.
Their lives are torn apart by the evil that has spread
and continues to spread in their homelands.

Your divine intervention is needed.

We pray that our world leaders can come together
and with Your help, find a solution to this problem.

Father, please heal all the broken pieces of humanity.
Help us to restore peace and hope in the shattered places of
Your world.
We need Your help. Please hear our prayers.

Amen.

Encouragement

Benevolent Father,

Not all days are filled with happy times.
There are times when nothing seems to be going right.
There is tension, chaos, worry, and fear.

Encourage us in times of defeat and weariness.
We can be beaten down and can feel overwhelmed.

Please uplift our spirits and help us to experience
the promise of Your abiding presence and love
when we are discouraged or downtrodden.

In our hour of need, You are there!
All we need to do is call on You.

Amen.

Differences

Loving Father,

We are such a curious people,
united in so many ways, yet divided in so many other ways.
We have different points of view and different perceptions
of the same situation.
You made us this way,
and perhaps the point of it is to learn from each other.
It would be a rather boring existence
if we lived in an environment of too much likeness.
Thank You for creating us this way.
In all this diversity, we still hold true to our core convictions of
faith in Jesus Christ.
Let's celebrate our love of Christ, and let's continue to hold true
to the belief that we can share our differences with each other
in a space that allows for us to be different and yet the same.

Amen.

Troubling Times Yet Again

Loving God,

History seems to repeat itself, and we find ourselves in the midst of much turmoil.

Why does evil continue to fester and grow?

We stand before You concerned and worried for our safety and for the safety of people in our country and across the globe.

There are so many events unfolding in this world that unsettle us.

We feel shocked by all of the unrest.

Butchery, barbarity, and malice are widespread.

We seek Your council, Lord, and we ask for Your intervention.

Help our leaders, from all over the world, to come together and solve this problem.

Let us all stand together and bring this savagery to an end.

Help Your people and let us feel Your presence.

Protect us all, Lord, we pray.

Amen.

Daybreak

Lord,

In the stillness of the early morning,
I come to commune with You,
my most gracious God.

What a magnificent world You have created.
I see the sunlight glistening on the trees.
Like the sunlight, I think of how Your presence
shines down on me and through me, invigorating my soul.

Oh what a joyful moment!

Amen.

Day's End

Beloved Father,

As we prepare to close this day,
may we look back at what has happened.
Did we honor You through our actions?
Did we remember to pray with You?
Did we give thanks for something as simple
as the sunshine or as grand as
an answered prayer?

We sang Your praises in preparation for Sunday services,
and You uplifted us with the sweet refrain of music and verse.

We take the anthems with us
and sing them to ourselves as we go about our lives.
This is a celebration of You in our hearts.
We love to sing Your praises.

Thank You for dwelling in our hearts
and responding to our songs.
This warms our hearts and uplifts our souls.
So we shall continue to sing Your praises during the day
and together in unison on Sunday in celebration of Your majesty.

You are a great and awesome God!

Amen.

Good Intentions

Dear Lord,

So many times our intentions do not match our performance.
We make plans to be more thankful and to spend more time with You in prayer.
We attempt to be kinder or to correct a long-established bad habit.
Then we trip, falling backward into old patterns.
Yet life goes on without our best intentions yielding good results.

Lord, You are so patient and loving with us.
Your encouraging voice can be heard reminding us
to begin anew and
to not be harsh with ourselves.
But change can happen. It begins with good intentions.

Little changes, here and there, do make a difference.
We hear You whispering in our hearts,
You can do it. I love the time you spend with Me doing My work.
Thank You, Father, for never giving up on us.

Amen.

Into This Day

O, dear Lord,
I pray I will go into this day with Your blessings.
Direct my steps.
Lead me where You wish me to go.
Serving You is my goal.

Amen.

Witnessing to Your Grace

Heavenly Father,

Draw us close to You.
Show us ways to bear witness to Your grace,
such as simple acts of kindness—
a smile, a hug,
or a word of encouragement.
Any act that uplifts someone, even briefly, serves You.
Love one another.
Be kind.
Be helpful.
Bless each other.
These are things You have taught us.
May we remember to act on them.

Amen.

2

Anytime Prayers

When you have a quiet moment in your day, connect with our Lord to share a thought or idea with Him.

Angels

Caring Father,
We give thanks for the angels
You have placed in our midst
to love, encourage, and protect us.
Some, in human form,
arrive in times when we are most vulnerable.
Others surround us from
Your heavenly kingdom above.

May we rest easy in their care.
Amen.

Be Still and Know That I Am

O, Father,
Too many times we say too much.
Fewer words might serve us well
as You showed us in Your statement,
"I am that I am."

May we reflect on this and know
Your presence is enough.
You envelop the universe.
We celebrate Your glory.

Amen.

Come into My Heart

Almighty God,

May we invite You into our hearts with this prayer:

I feel Your presence in my life.
I see the good, the harmony, and the
beauty of the moment.

As You watch over me,
may I listen intently for Your direction.

Thank You, Lord, for all You have given me.

Amen.

Destructive Patterns

Lord,

Too easily we fall into destructive patterns,
wasting precious time and energy on things
that are not in harmony with Your goals for our lives.
Save us from our lost ways, Redeemer God.
Set us right. Keep urging us forward.

Amen.

Forgive Me When I Whine

Heavenly Father,

So many times my prayers to You are filled with
"I need this. I want that. Help me. If only You would
give me this, I could have a much better life."

Some of these needs are great;
the problems or illnesses we bring to You are real and painful.
You want us to bring our concerns to You in prayer.
But we disappoint You, Lord, when we spend the majority of
our prayer time asking for or demanding something.

If we stepped back and looked at ourselves, we might see
unhappy children.
Let us strive to balance prayer times with moments of simple
communing with You
or by offering expressions of gratitude and wonderment for all
of Your creation.

You long for these times with us.
You enrich us in these moments,
warming our souls in wondrous ways.

Amen.

Grateful Hearts

Loving God,

You are magnificent—
from creation to a promise so big it is boundless.
Easter has passed, but the promise of salvation
and eternal life are here with us forever.
We could repeat that message over and over,
and it would never get old.

So we stand before You with grateful hearts.
You have filled us with hope that shall never fade.
Lead us, Lord, where You wish us to go.
Keep us ever mindful of that hope
as we live our lives.

Amen.

Not All Days Are Light and Bright

Merciful God,

Not all days are light and bright
or carefree and easy.
Oh, how we wish they were.

In these times when sadness seems to envelope us,
comfort us, Lord, with Your caring hand.
Assure us of Your unconditional love.

Lift us up.

Amen.

Open Our Hearts

Loving God,

Open our hearts to receive Your grace.
Please pardon our selfish inclinations.
Soften our will to be more receiving of Your peace.

Amen

Open Us to Your Teachings

Loving God,

What is Your will for our lives?

So often we veer off course,
a little too far to the right or to the left on the path of life.
We become too narrow-minded.

We wrap ourselves up in our own interests or concerns.

Help us become more open to Your teachings.
You have asked us to love You,
to love our neighbors,
and to be more kind and generous of heart.
Stretch us in those directions.

Open us to the possibility of loving boldly in Your name.

Amen.

Our Part in the Vastness of Creation

Omnipresent God,

We kneel before You and honor You.
Your creation spreads out before us.
We stand in awe of the magnitude of the small part we are able to comprehend.
In the vastness of creation, You chose mankind to be Your children.
A gift so large, it humbles us.

We lack the understanding to grasp the magnitude of this gift.
But one thing is certain: We do understand and feel the love You wrap around us.

Maybe it is enough—
or a beginning for now.

Amen.

Special Gifts and Connectedness

Loving God,

You created each and every one of us and have given us unique and special gifts.
No two of us are exactly alike, not even identical twins.

You placed us in a family and a community to flourish and enrich each other.
While caring and being cared for, sharing with others and having them share with us, and loving and being loved back, we are all connected in Your divine plan.

Do we know how much of a difference each of us makes?
You long for us to know our value and preciousness in Your sight.
In this time of quiet reflection and prayer,
fill us with Your love, peace, and the knowledge.
We are unique and special gifts, not only to You but also to the world.

We feel Your love and Your soft, gentle hand upon our shoulders.
We are blessed indeed by Your presence here with us.

Amen.

The Melody of Life

Heavenly Father,

You gave us the melody of life,
and it is a sweet refrain.
It sweeps us along in harmony with the world,
and life is good, and all is well.
But then, on occasion, we start to sing off-key.

What happened?

We lose sight of that melody,
and life becomes a bumpy path.
We are not sure how it went wrong.
Is there that much to distract us? Is that it?
Did an old injury resurface, and we reacted in old ways?

We search for the melody,
and it seems to have disappeared.
We become anxious, angry, and maybe even cynical.
Oh what a world, how wrong things seem to be going.

How did we end up here?

At these times, we need to pull back,
shut out that off-key melody,
remain still in God's presence, and wait.

Ask for help.
Surrender.
Wait and wait some more.

Oh, what is that we hear?
Yes, it is the sweet refrain of the melody of life filling us with song.

Amen.

The Seed of Faith

Lord,

You planted within each of us a seed of faith—
a belief in something intangible and unseen.
A stirring in our souls confirms its presence.

You are in us, and we are in You.
Take comfort from this knowledge.

You are not alone.
God enfolds you in His Love.

Amen.

The Warmth of Your Love

Heavenly Father,

Oh to walk into the sunshine of Your presence and
to stand in the warmth of Your love
I am filled with hope
and open to the possibilities this day holds for me.

May I shine like the beam of Your light that surrounds me.

Amen.

The Vastness of Creation

Magnificent God, Creator of all that is known and unknown,
we celebrate Your power and glory.

Your vastness is so large,
we can't comprehend the magnitude of it all.
Yet here, we are but a tiny speck in it, and You are watching
over us.
Always accessible to us, Your love surrounds us.

Amen.

Your Presence in Our Lives

Gracious Lord,

Open our hearts to Your urgings.
Help us be more connected to You.

Direct us in ways to serve You.
As You have said,
"Be still and feel My presence at work in you."

Help us take quiet moments throughout the day
to connect with You, to center ourselves,
and to glorify You.

Amen.

Morning

Heavenly Father,

As we look to the morning and sit in the beginning of a new day,
may we take a few moments to focus on You.

Take us into the new day filled with Your love,
ready to face the challenges we know await us
and mindful that You walk beside us.

All is well with our souls.

Amen.

Preparing the Feast to Come

Loving God,

We praise Your holy name and give thanks for all that You have in store for us
when the world is removed of sin, disease, poverty,
injustice, misery, oppression, and death
and restored with love, joy, merrymaking, singing, dancing,
and eating at the feast You have prepared for us.

We look forward to seeing those who have gone before us and those we have lost contact with.

We will celebrate with our family and friends and all of Your children.
There will be peace, harmony, laughter, and great joy—a mighty celebration.

We ask, Lord, that You fortify us and send us out into this world eager and
ready to make the changes that will bring Your plan to fruition.

Bless and guide us.

Thank You for bringing us together to love and support each other.
Embolden us now to take Your love out into the community.

Amen.

A Deacon's Meeting Prayer

Almighty and most gracious God,

As we bring our meeting to a close, we thank You for our church
and the opportunity to serve as deacons.
May we be mindful of our congregation's needs,
and may our actions serve to welcome and enhance
our focus on the church and in the larger community.

Please bless our church leaders and our congregation.
May we share, with all those we encounter, the love
You have so richly given to us.

May our church be a beacon in the community, drawing people
closer to You
and enriching their understanding of You and Your purpose for
their lives.

Please bless each person present, giving all a sense of purpose
as they seek to better glorify You.

Amen.

3

Prayers for Renewal

Traditionally, the beginning of each year affords us the opportunity to reflect on our blessings and what we hope to accomplish in the coming year. But renewal can occur at any time and is not limited to the beginning of a new year.

The prayers offered here are to help focus and center us, as we go forward, on thanksgiving and hope. Living in gratitude and being open to the possibilities in our lives begins with acknowledgement and petition to our Lord as we seek His guidance. We are grateful to Him for the lessons and blessings He has provided to us. These prayers may help you consider the question: What does community mean to me?

A Bright New Year

Loving Father,

A new year dawns before us. Our spirits soar.
We look heavenward and lift our praises to You,
most dear and beloved God.
You have so richly blessed us.

How should we spend our time in this new year?

Let's begin by drawing close to You.
Let us look to Your teachings for direction.

Oh, the opportunities present in the gifts
You have placed before us—
gifts we can enjoy and share.
Let us begin!

Amen.

A New Year Begins

Heavenly Father,
As this new year begins, we contemplate what it portends.
We hope for peace in our world
but do not feel optimistic it will come anytime soon.

The news is filled with struggle and strife, both at home and aboard.
What are we to do?
Can we make a difference?

Show us the way, Lord.

Amen.

Into the New Year We Go

Our radiant and most gracious God,

In this new year, may we resolve to spend more time
with You in quiet prayer and reflection.

We ask that You guide us in how we might serve You.
Please open our hearts to the lessons You have given to each
of us.
May we learn and grow from these lessons so we will become
the beacons of light You wish us to be.

Please bless us Lord.

May we go out into the world with the love
and the peace of the blessings You have bestowed upon us,
so that we might share these blessings with all those we meet.

Amen.

January Begins

Loving God,

A new year has begun.
We are filled with resolutions
and thoughts of what this year will hold for us.

Let us begin the year with a spirit of gratitude.
Keep us focused on You and lead us
in the direction You wish us to follow.

Help us spend more time with You each day.
May we honor You in those sacred moments.

Please hear our prayers to You—the ones delivered aloud
and also those offered to You in silence.

In closing, Lord, we ask that You please watch over us
and illuminate the path before us.

Amen.

Joy in the Moment

Loving God,

How many times do we miss opportunities to live in joy?
When we look around, what do we see?
A beautiful place to live? An abundance of food?
Perhaps the freedom to walk out into the day and go wherever
we wish?
Certainly, these things should bring us joy.

Help us not to be so diverted by daily pressures
that we overlook what is right in front of us.

There are joys, big and small, present all around us—
joys just waiting to be discovered
and for us to take pleasure in them.

They are reminders of Your love.
We thank You for the many joys
You have bestowed upon us.

Amen.

New Year Beginnings

Loving God,

As a new year dawns, we expectantly look ahead
and wonder what You have planned for us.

Are we up to the task?
Will our hearts burst with joy,
or will we fail to find the gifts You have placed before us?

Sometimes we miss the obvious and often the subtle, as well.
Stir us with the new awareness that we might become the people
You planned us to become, all the while celebrating
and delighting in Your wonder and compassion.

Amen.

New Year Invitation

Heavenly Father,

As we begin the new year, draw us close to You.
Let us feel Your presence in our lives.

Strengthen our resolve to be kinder and more loving people.
May we take time each day to engage You in prayer
and to express our gratitude for all the blessings You have
bestowed upon us.

We have so much to be thankful for.
Keep us on the right path.
Help us to make choices reflective of our love for You.

Amen.

A Fresh Start

Almighty God,

As this new year begins,
we are filled with many hopes and plans
to make our lives more meaningful, prosperous, and healthy.

The new year is a fresh beginning.
We are optimistic about what it will hold.
You are ever present, cheering us on and eager to be a part of
all of our plans.

May we strive to start our day in quiet conversation with You.
May we give thanks for our blessings.
May we ask for help with our needs.
May we focus on the opportunities, each day holds, to share
Your love
and encourage those around us.
May we always remember You are here with us in every moment.

Amen.

4

Prayers for Strength

During trials and struggles, when all seems hopeless, we can access our Lord through prayer. We are not alone and can renew ourselves by reaching out to our Lord. He will strengthen us. We need only to come before Him, share our pain, and ask for His help. He will bring us comfort.

Being Passive

O Lord,
It is so much easier to be passive.
When I hesitate, push me forward.

Embolden me to step up, to speak up,
and to do the right thing.

Don't let me shy away from action.

Amen.

Deep in Despair

Our Lord,

Sometimes when deep in despair,
we feel separated from You.
Dark thoughts fill our heads.
We don't know which way to turn,
and deep within, there is a sense of being alone.

Cold, sad, empty silence seems to surround us.

"Help!" we cry out.
"Save us from this deep, foreboding place.
Draw us close to You. Lift this veil of despair."

Hear our pleas. We wait on You, Lord.

Amen.

Keep Me Centered

Heavenly Father,

Distractions here, distractions there,
distractions are everywhere.
How easily we are pulled away from
what is truly meaningful in our lives.

How do we stay centered on Jesus?
What can we do?
Implementing a new and simple act
could put us on a new path.
When we wake in the morning, before anything else,
we could welcome Jesus into the new day.
We could give Him thanks for what the day will bring,
always trusting in His abundant love.

Keep me centered, Father.

Amen.

Loneliness

Dear Lord,

During the times of struggle and sadness in our lives,
we pull away from You in despair.
Why do we do this?

Dark places envelop us.
Loneliness isolates us, and the pain is great.

Lord, help lift us up when we feel helpless.
Leave us not to our own devices.
Draw us close to You and
comfort us with Your nurturing love.

Amen.

Not All Days Are Light and Bright

Merciful God,

Not all days are light and bright or carefree and easy.
Oh, how we wish they were.

When times of sadness seem to envelop us,
comfort us, Lord, with Your caring hand.
Assure us of Your unconditional love.

Lift us up.

Amen.

Pain and Despair

Father,

In the darkness of despair,
I raise a call up to You, O Lord.
This mortal journey is not always easy.
More times than we care to mention,
sadness and disappointment attempt to consume us.
Why are there dark paths and disappointments?
I cannot find the reason,
although I continue to search.

Why does it elude me,
almost delighting in my pain?
I am reaching for You, Lord.
I'm seeking understanding.

I won't let go of Your hand.
Please beam Your light on this dark place.
I sense You will not rescue me
until I achieve understanding of this situation.

I know You are here with me.
See my tears and feel my pain.

Amen.

Sadness

Loving God,

Sometimes we are in pain.
Our souls are troubled, and we cry
deep within ourselves.
While no tears are in our eyes,
they still burn deep within our souls.

There are no words to express what we feel.
Comfort us in these dark, trying times.
Pull us out of despair.

Lift us up, dear Lord, lift us up.

Amen.

Stand Up

Yes, yes, Lord,

Sometimes I hear You calling me:
"Stand up.
Do the right thing.
Look beyond yourself."

Do I answer the call?
Have I been the good steward?
Do I heed Your instructions?
Sadly, I don't always do this.
I trip, I fail, and I ignore.

Forgive me and help me stand
strong on the side of righteousness.

Amen.

Tears of Sadness

My Father,

My heart is breaking with sadness.
The pain is deep and raw.
How did this happen?

I feel cold, alone, and separated from You.
Life seems hollow, and cynicism
pulls me down.

How could this be? What went so
terribly wrong? Wounded and sad, I
sit in the dark and cry.

O Lord, deliver me!

Amen.

The Broken Place

Merciful Father,

You know our hearts as if they were open books.
You see our pain, our worry, and our concerns.
We know we shouldn't be fearful,
and yet, we are.

Please come into the broken places.
Dwell with us in the scary times
when we are so discouraged.
Open us to the possibilities and
show us solutions, if there are solutions.
If there aren't any, please give us
the understanding that some things will not change
no matter how much we pray for a different outcome.

In these dark times, one thing is certain:
Your love is present, and You are with us.
May we hold onto that one constant, which is You.
We know You will never forsake us.
We know that, beyond the darkness of this time,
there will be a dawn rising, which will be filled with hope and
renewal.

Amen.

Times of Despair

Heavenly Father,

In times of trouble and sadness,
we feel so cold and alone.
We are alone and dejected.
Where are You, Lord?
It is we who have pulled away from You,
yet we confuse this separation as something You've done.

Life is not always easy. In fact,
much of it can be a trial.
The challenges can be daunting.
We have failed and stand ravaged
by sickness and losses of many kinds.
With heavy hearts, we retreat into despair.

But wait. You are with us. We are not alone!
Ever so slowly, the veil of pain is lifted.
The sorrow disappears. You were present.

You are present.
We are safe.

We give You thanks for
Your abiding and steadfast love.
Please, Lord, lead us to a
place of peace and harmony.

Amen.

Turmoil

Loving God,

These are times of struggle and turmoil.
Uncertainty is everywhere in our country
and around the world.

People are concerned for
their own lives and those of their families.
How did this become a universal problem?

Even in the midst of chaos, You are present.
We know You have a Divine plan for
each of us and for Your world.

Draw us close to You. Help us stay focused on
You and not become lost in worry or despair.
Calm our fears and surround us with Your peace.

Amen.

Weary of the Journey

Almighty God,

We come to You at
times of struggle in our lives.
We weary of the journey. What are we to do?

We listen for Your voice. In this moment of
stillness, speak to us, guide us, and encourage us.

Amen.

5

Prayers for Peace

At our very cores is a desire for peace—peace in our hearts, in our families, in our communities, and yes, in our world. It begins by centering ourselves in God's presence. We then can reach out to our communities and work for peace there.

What can we do in our communities to effect positive change? Beyond this, what can we do for our country and then the world? It begins with our connection to God and grows from there. We might think that this is all too grand a plan. But it is God's plan, and it begins with each of us. If we focus on beginning to and letting God lead us, amazing things can happen.

Seeking Peace

Heavenly Father,

Draw us close to You.
Warm us with Your presence.
Still the turmoil that threatens our tranquility
and replace it with a sense of peace.

Your peace is something that cannot be moved or altered.
It is a perfect peace,
a pure peace,
a never-changing peace,
and an ever-perfect peace.

Amen.

Peace in My Soul

Heavenly Father,

At the end of another day,
we seek Your presence.
Draw us close to You, Lord.
Fill us with the peace that will nourish our souls.
Lift, from us, the weariness we feel.
Refresh us with Your warmth and love.
Hold us close.

How safe we feel in Your refuge.
Oh, that we could remain in this place,
that we would not lose sight of the fact
You are ever-present in our lives.

We need only to call upon You to reconnect,
no matter where we are or what we are doing.
We must step out of the ordinary
into the extraordinary—
the place where You abide.

Amen.

Peace in Our Hearts

Loving God,

Grant that we might find
peace in our hearts.
Give us a stillness and connectedness
to You in solitude.
We seek a time of quiet
where we may share our hearts with You.

The world can be so turbulent.
We often feel tossed about
and not fully centered.

Hold us close, Lord. Fill us
with Your all-encompassing love.
Warm and renew us so we feel energized
and ready to go out into the world
calmer and at peace.

Amen.

Peace on Earth

Father,

Peace on earth—what is my part in this?

It all begins with one person
and grows as one becomes two
and two becomes three,
until an army of God's people are
marching and spreading good deeds.

Could this change the world?
Think about it. Could it change your marriage, family,
church, community, state, country, or world?
Is it possible? Look what Jesus did!

Let's try.

Amen.

6

Prayers for Reconciliation

With so much turmoil and static in our world, we need to step back and refocus on what is truly important in our lives. These prayers offer a way to center ourselves, to regroup, and to move forward in peace.

Common Ground

Our Lord,

Let us find common ground—
a place where we can stand in
Your presence as brothers and sisters.
You have given us a community of faith.

May we espouse the ideals You have taught us.
Bring us together, heal our divisions, and join us
in a common thread of godly understanding.

Amen.

Distractions

Heavenly Father,

In this world of instant news, we easily become distracted
from the truly meaningful things in life.
There is so much chaos around us.

Please calm the chatter in our heads.
Direct us to a place of peace where
truly meaningful things in life become apparent.
Help us to step back and refocus, placing our eyes on Jesus.

If we stand in silence with You,
You will fill us with tranquility.
Then we can begin anew
with a sense of calm and purpose.

Amen.

Election

Heavenly Father,

The election is over. It was a long fought battle for each side.
Some are terribly disappointed, and others are jubilant.

The people have spoken, and now we need to unite and work
together.
Are we willing to do our part?
Our elected leaders have expressed a willingness to work together.
We pray for them and hope they can stay the course.

Please give us the wisdom to know that
mutual cooperation is the road to solving problems.
Open us to this and keep us from returning to the
old ways, which have failed to produce solutions.
We must stop believing that one way
is the only or best way.
Let's seek compromise.

We can do great things if we work together.
Unite us Lord
and heal the divides.

Move us forward.
Now is the time.
Now is the place.
Help us stand together and move forward.

Amen.

Hardheartedness

Father,

We have lost our civility. Hard lines have been drawn
and stiff positions have been taken.
Guard us from hardheartedness. Break through the wall
that separates us from each other.

We can be so stiff, firm, and unyielding
that we shut people out. We judge each other
and are so sure of what is right,
we become deaf to what is being said.

Surely this is not what You intended.

Soften our posture, open our hearts,
and help us hear what is being said.
We don't need to agree with one another.
But we might learn a thing or two from each other
if we just listened.

This week, let us pray for situations
that will open us to this possibility.
Embolden us to be brave enough to try.
Let us explore and seek opportunities to see
something new or from a different prospective.
The possibilities are exciting.

Amen.

7

Prayers for Contemplation

In this fast-paced world of ours, we may find that we do not take the time to quietly reflect on what is happening in our world. Do we take time to step back and consider how our actions impact others? What is our impact on the world? We all occupy a sacred space. Do we live as if we understand this?

Busyness of the World

Loving God,

Please take us away from
the busyness of this world.
We need quiet time with You.

Let us join You in a time of contemplation
to examine our lives and actions.
Let us explore ways to
glorify You, to honor You,
and to share Your powerful message of
love and forgiveness with one and all.

Let us commit to pray about this and
to listen for Your direction.
Let us also commit to take action
when the opportunity presents itself.

May we serve You, Lord.

Amen.

Fainthearted

Loving God,

How often do we become discouraged and fainthearted or
feel defeated before we even begin?

Why is this?

Cynicism is ever ready to pull us down.
All around us there is so much to feel sad about.
How do we lift ourselves up?

A good starting point is by spending time
with You each day and giving thanks for
all the goodness in our lives.

Strengthen our resolve to include You
throughout our days, from the little moments
to lengthier times of contemplation and prayer.

We will do our best to commit to this process.
An ongoing conversation with You, throughout the day,
will certainly lead us to a more positive feeling within.

We are surrounded by Your presence, and
as Your love warms our very souls,
we thank You.

Thank You for Your eternal presence.
Thank You for Your constant caring.
We welcome these times with You.

Amen.

In Search of Understanding

Our loving God,

We come before You in search of understanding.
The lessons, which spring forth in our daily lives,
are opportunities to help purify our souls.

Our failings and mistakes, when recognized and corrected,
prepare us for lives that are more deeply pondered.
The growth in our understanding deepens our wisdom.
It is the gift of these lessons.

What a journey we are on, Lord.
Oh, that we won't let these lessons pass us by!

Amen.

Miracles in the Moment

Loving God,

Oh, how the busyness of the day
can pull us away from You.
But if we are still, we can reconnect with You
and witness a little miracle occurring.

In a time of prayer with You, we feel the divine connection.
You cause a flutter in our beings—
a reminder that You and we are one.

Oh, that we might hold that moment
and keep it at the forefront of our consciousness,
instilling the calm of sublime connectedness with You.

Embrace us, Lord, that we might, in turn, embrace You.
Thank You for Your ever-present love.

Amen.

Missed Opportunities

Heavenly Father,

In our daily lives, You present us with lessons to be learned.
They can appear suddenly, unexpectedly,
and sometimes, subtly.

These failings and mistakes,
when recognized and corrected,
prepare us for a life more deeply pondered.

Is not it Your goal for us to learn
from these opportunities?
Growing spiritually through these challenges
deepens our wisdom and are the gifts of these lessons.

Oh, that we do not miss the opportunities
present in each day.

Amen.

Quiet Time with Our Lord

Dear Lord,

May we step out of ourselves
and into a place of silence before You.
We are waiting, watching,
and anticipating Your presence.
We invite You and Your welcoming of us.
We relish the peace that comes over us.

Regarding the envelopment of Your love,
nothing needs to be said.
Just spend time together
and be peaceful and comforting.

We acknowledge that we are Yours.
Blessed be the tie that binds!

Amen.

The Reality of Life

Heavenly Father,

Oh, this reality we call life.
Why is there suffering, disease, and death?
Now that is a ponderable question.

If You gave us the answer,
could we comprehend it? Perhaps not,
and yet we wonder about the
meaning of it all and what
our place is in it?

We seek our place in Your divine plan
but often feel we are not securely planted in it.
Is this a question of perception?

We are not truly grasping the full picture.
Pull us in, Lord. Help us find our footing, we pray.

Amen.

Repentance

Almighty God,

Humbly we stand before You, confessing we are not
behaving in harmony with Your teachings.
We are proud, boastful, and unyielding.
We offer excuses for actions
that reinforce our posturing.
Yet these defenses fall short.

We are such stubborn people.

Please help us to redirect our focus.
Speak to us in ways we can understand.
It may be different for each of us.

Sharpen our minds and hearts to Your direction.
Yes, Lord, we are willing.
Sometimes, it is simply that we do not always act
on what we know is right.

Amen.

Sharing Time

Wondrous Lord,

Please encourage us to make
an effort, in the coming days,
to take a few moments each day
and spend them with You—perhaps a
quiet, reflective time with You
to ponder something in Your creation.

It could be something simple like a flower
or vast like the Milky Way.

It could be a conversation with You,
where we express our awe and appreciation
of what we are examining.

We know You welcome these times of fellowship.
We can almost hear You say,
"Come and sit with me. I want to hear your thoughts."

Who knows? You might just whisper back,
filling us with Your warmth and promise.

Amen.

Trust

Heavenly Father,

May we trust You completely.
Guide us to sort out what is important and unimportant in our lives.
Instill in us a resolve to spend more time with You each day.
This would ideally be a time away from the noise and distractions of this world.
It would be a quiet time where You will enrich us with Your warmth and love.

If we listen, You will help us crystallize a view of our lives
as You intended them to be—filled with contentment, prosperity, and hope.

We are in such need during difficult times.
Left to our own devices,
we fret over the challenges
in our personal lives, whether it is sickness,
loved ones in distress, financial worries,
job insecurity, job loss, or even death.

These challenges are real, and we are in pain.
We know You will intercede when we ask You.
Therefore, Lord, we ask for Your intercession.
Please hear our prayers.
Envelop us in Your peace.

Amen.

Universal Truth

Magnificent God,

Looking at the night sky, we realize
that this universe could be one of many.
In our universe, there are billions of galaxies,
in the center of which rests Your presence.

You preside over all that is known and unknown.
We look to the night sky and see the beauty and
the wonder of it all.

Yet we see so little.

Let us fall on our knees and praise You
for selecting us to be Your much-loved children.
Right in the center of this vastness rests
our relationship with You.

So honored are we.
So privileged are we.
All honor and glory we give to Thee.

Amen.

8

Prayers for Involvement

Jesus instructed us to go out and be His messengers in the world and to bring the good news to all those we come in contact with. This can be done in big and small ways. We can each make a difference by doing whatever we can to share God's love.

Do I Hear You When You Are Calling?

Ever-present God,

Do we hear when You are calling?
Are we mindful of how You might present Yourself to us?
The opportunities come many times a day.

When we see a downtrodden person,
do we smile and say hello?
Do we listen when a friend is discouraged?
Do we join a community project?
Do we stand up to injustice or simply turn away?
Help us disconnect from the excuse of being
too busy to get involved.

Every day, all the time,
You are showing us ways to share Your love.
Open our eyes to the possibilities
and nudge us to respond.

We may never know how we changed
a person's life or a situation by our actions.
But we do change things in big and small ways
when we do Your work.

The time is now, and it all begins with us.
So let us wait no more.

Amen.

Earthquakes and Calamities

Loving God,

As we approach Your throne,
our hearts are filled with concerns for this world.
Calamities continue to convulse our planet.
We see the fury of nature devastate so many places
through earthquakes, tsunamis, and further tragedies, such as
in Japan
when a nuclear power plant melted down,
resulting in the spread of radiation.

We see unrest spreading across the Middle East.
Libya is in revolt, and the people are risking everything
to bring freedom, social justice, and opportunity to their country.
The people of Libya appeal for help.
But the world sits by as people die.
They look to the United States

What are we to do?

We need Your direction.
We give thanks to You for all You have given us
in this beautiful, abundant country of America.
You have blessed us with so much.

We are reminded, however, that
to those to whom much is given,
much is also expected.

May we lead the way, but may it be a joint effort
with all the countries of the world.

Amen.

Elections

Loving Lord,

How contentious our elections have become.
Let us do our part by being mindful of Your teachings
as we make our decisions.
May we all vote our consciences, and when the results are in,
may we work together to move our country forward.
That work begins with restoring reason and civility in our public discourse
and letting our elected officials know we expect the same from them.

End the reign of bitterness and divisiveness,
which has consumed the
public debate and governmental proceedings.
Work through us to restore a sense of the common good
and quiet the voices that would tear us apart.

We believe in the words of our Pledge of Allegiance—
that we are one nation under God.
We ask Your help in reconnecting to one another,
even when differing points of view divide us.

Our work begins with small steps—our steps.
May You help us rebuild this country and restore
it's founding principles of liberty and justice for all.

Amen.

Eternal Struggle

Heavenly Father,

Sometimes we are just plain tired of this world—
its conflicts, corruption, and the
callous disregard for others.

These things are nothing new. They have been around
since the beginning of time.
They have played out from
biblical times through present day.

A person faces struggles no matter
what his or her station is in life.
We know it is the eternal struggle
between good and evil.
So the burning question is:
What would You have us do, Lord?

We will pray and await Your answer.

Amen.

Evil in the World

Merciful Father,

Evil is alive and well, dwelling among us and
seeking an opportunity to strike. This we have seen
with the bombings in Boston.

Sadly, this is an everyday occurrence in our world,
although not usually so close to home.
Many live with the reality of bombs
dropping all around them.
We cannot even imagine what enduring the
daily terror of such an existence would be like.

We pray to You, Lord, for help.
Not only as people of the
United States but as citizens of the world.
Help us root out evil and bring Your
blessings of peace and love to all who seek it.

This is not an easy task.
We are overwhelmed just thinking about
what to do and how to do it.

We fear we are too small to make a difference.
So show us what we can do, individually and in groups.
Let the work toward peace continue to grow from there.

We ask that You protect us, Lord,
and lead us where You will.
We await Your word.

Amen.

Stop the Terrorists

Heavenly Father,

We have all been saddened by the threats and acts of extreme violence
and the use of intimidation becoming a part of our daily reality.
People were going about their lives, enjoying themselves, and celebrating
and then, suddenly, were cut down by terrorists. We shake our heads
and are unable to understand this hatred.

We ask for Your intervention. Help the world come together
to stop terrorism. Help our leaders to find a way to root out the
problems, which draw people to be radicalized.

You gave us this beautiful planet, rich in such splendor and
diversity. Help us to bring people together to live in peace
and prosperity, to end the violence, and to honor You.

Be with us, Lord, root out evil, heal the divides, and bring
peace on earth, we pray.

Amen.

Natural Disasters

Almighty God,

Weekly, we hear of natural disasters destroying parts of our country.
We pray for those who have lost so much in the havoc of the storms.
May You bring them comfort and hope
as they rebuild their lives.
Thank You for the brave people who came to help and to rescue them.
The best part of humanity shows itself in times of disaster.

May the spirit of togetherness and caring linger
in the aftermath of the storms, forever reminding us
we are all connected and joined together in
Your holy family.

Amen.

Making the World
a Better Place

Almighty God,

Could we change the world or our place in it
by just offering fellow travelers a smile?
A compliment?
A hug or a helping hand?

It feels good to be
on the receiving end of this arrangement.
It also feels good to be
on the giving end of this arrangement.

To carry the point further, it makes You, our God,
happy when You witness this occurrence.

Wasn't the message to love one another?

We know there is much work needed in this area and
on a much larger scale.
But for now, perhaps we can concentrate on
this time, this space,
and our place in it.

Keep us open to opportunities to share Your love.
Allow us to accept Your love.
Let us be mindful of how it feels
to be surrounded by and a part of that love.
It is such a gift, and blessed are we
who have received it.

Amen.

Serving a Higher Good

Heavenly Father,

Teach us to become humble servants
who seek a higher good and
help those in need.
Help us perform simple of acts of kindness
as part of our day.

May we look for opportunities
to share Your love with others.
Little actions can make differences.
Bold actions make even bigger differences.

Wherever we are in our journey,
may You reveal to us Your will
so that we might make You proud by our actions.

You have given us so many blessings.
Thank You for opening us to the
possibility of sharing them with others.

Amen.

Tinderbox World

Heavenly Father,

What a tinderbox our world has become,
inflamed with anger and rage.
We see people rising up
in the streets across the Middle East.
Here at home, we look on in surprise and disbelief.
Where is all this headed?

We tremble at the possibilities.
Lord, we need Your help to calm the unrest.
Please guide our world leaders as they address
the underlying problems. We pray for Your intervention
as new governments emerge.

When broken down to the most common denominators,
people want the same things:
safe places to live and worship,
opportunities to work and shelter their families,
and to live in peace.

Are these possible? We ask for Your intervention.
Lord, hear our prayers.

Amen.

Listening to God

Loving God,

As we fast, pray, and seek understanding,
we wait on You, Lord.

What can I do?
What will please You?
Keep me focused, listening for Your direction.
Help me not shy away from
my responsibilities as a follower of Jesus.

This is an individual prayer in a group setting.
It begins with me and grows into the community.
It must start with me, and the time is now.

Lead me forward.

Amen.

Changing World

Lord God, Master of all,

We sense that things are changing in our world.
There is struggle, grief, and strife on one side,
and a call to address those concerns on the other.
The challenge is great and resistance is mounting.
Many reasons are offered to just stand silent and not act:
"It is not our problem.
It will cost too much in terms of personal commitment
or even national commitment for that matter."

Yet, You have called us to action through Your teachings.
It is not enough to simply be good, honest, God-fearing people.
You have called for us to act.

So, Lord, how are we to do this?
Encourage us to pray on this.
Urge us in silent moments to listen for Your voice.
Let us keep our hearts and minds open to
ways of serving You in our daily life.

Amen.

The Drumbeat Continues

Almighty God,

We hear the drumbeat in the distance.
Change is in the air.
Wait, have we not already prayed about this before?
Yes, but what have we done?

Things are being unsettled in order to be set
on a more firm foundation.
This change is bold and loud
yet also subtle and soft.
It is everywhere.
Are we going to be part of this change?
Or will we watch it pass by?

You are trying to get our attention.
Could the violence in nature be part of our awakening?
Did You not use whirlwinds, earthquakes, and floods,
in the distant past, to get our attention?

Yes, even the cry from humanity is rising.
Many of us are comfortable and like our lives.
A good life is a good thing.
We are thankful for our blessings, even when
we do not always praise You for them.
Still, this is not enough.

On some level, we all know this is true.
Our church elders and national leaders are calling for change.
We ask that You open our minds
and instill the willingness to do our part.
Show us the way and push us to action.

We are aware of the criticism mounting in our heads
to resist doing the right thing.
Were we not warned of Satan's presence?
He is ever eager to lull us into complacency
so he may go about causing suffering and unrest in the world.
Would he not use our inaction to perpetuate his aims?

These are things for us to think about, Lord.
Yes indeed!

Amen.

To Whom Much Is Given

Loving God,

You have blessed us so abundantly
and have given us so many reasons to thank You.
How can we show our appreciation?
What would You have us do?

We could start by making Your presence known through
anonymous acts of kindness.
We could do the smallest things
to make a difference.

The world would be so much better
if each of us developed an attitude of
gratefulness and a willingness to share
our blessings with others.

Encourage us, Lord, to begin right now.
Let's see where You lead us!

Amen.

Trip and Fall

Our Father,

Over and over, we trip and fall.
Sometimes it seems there are
so many mistakes and wrong turns in our lives.

We could have been kinder.
We could have done more.
We could have borne witness
But instead,
we stood silent and did nothing.

When will we ever learn?
How human we are, indeed.

Tomorrow awaits, and with it
there is an opportunity to try a little harder.
Little by little, change is possible,
so forward we go.

Hope is eternal.

Amen.

Turn the Other Cheek

Father,

You taught us to strive
to live by the highest principles
of our faith's traditions:
to respect all people
and to love all people.
This is a very challenging goal.

Encourage us when we feel we can't do it
and turn away from the challenge.

You turned Your cheek.
Help us to turn ours toward what's right—
even as we resist.
Amen.

Your Love Spilling over Me

Radiant God,

Like sunshine splashing on our faces,
Your love spills over us,
enveloping us in warmth and caring.
May we take that love into the world
and share it with others.
Let us share, care, and celebrate You at every opportunity.

Let those we meet see, feel, and
take it with them.
Thank You, Jesus.
We welcome the opportunities
to share Your love!

Amen.

9

Seasonal Prayers

Oh, the joy that greets us each year as we relive, with reflection and celebration, our Lord Jesus's life journey. His teachings and miracles are on display for all to see. We learn so much from Him. Let us strive to follow His examples.

Advent Journey

Loving God,

The star shone forth in the eastern sky,
illuminating the path of the three wise men.
What could they have been thinking?

As we journey on the Advent path,
what are we thinking?
What fears and hopes linger in our hearts?

Lord, You know all our secrets that rest there.
Please take us by the hand and guide us.
Prepare our hearts for the coming of Jesus.

Thank You, Father, for Your ever-abiding presence
and for Your promise of perfect peace and joy.

Amen.

Fall Reflections

Dear Lord,

As the days grow shorter
and we see leaves turning color and
falling from the trees, there is a stillness
that welcomes contemplation.

This is a time for reflection. Be with us
in these quiet moments, Lord.
Guide us to a better understanding
of what Your plan is for each of us.

Amen.

Lent

Loving God,

As we begin this Lenten season,
may we find moments in each day to spend with You—
moments to reflect upon the struggle
and sacrifice Jesus made for our salvation.

Let us reflect on how we might serve You better
and purify our thoughts and deeds.
Speak to us in these quite moments
and guide our actions.

Amen.

Lent and Our Purpose

Almighty God,

What would You have us do
in this Lenten season?
Give up something dear to us?
Fast? Pray? Purify our hearts?

We desire to do Your will.
Help us take time each day to be with You
and to listen to and seek Your guidance.
These quiet times of reflection in Your presence enrich us.
Speak to us, Lord. Open our hearts to receive Your word.

May this Lenten season be one where
we actively seek to be connected to You.

Amen.

Lenten Prayer

Loving God,

Speak to us in this time of prayer.
Renew in us a resolve to be
more mindful of Your call.
Heal the parts of us that are broken.
Uplift our spirits and lead us
to a place of peace and serenity.

We invite You to dwell within our hearts.
Lead us where You will.
We await Your guidance.

Amen.

Lenten Season 1

Almighty, living God,

The dark days and trials are remembered in
the days of Lent.
The sinister side of humanity revealed itself
in the days leading up to the Crucifixion.
The easy way out was rejected.

Can we even grasp the sacrifice Jesus made for our sins?
In this time of reflection and remembrance,
may we honestly confess how undeserving we feel,
and how we continue to falter and
make the same mistakes again and again.

Draw us to You, Lord.
Hear our confessions
and our silent prayers as we offer them to You.
Even now, we have so much more we could add.

On each of these days leading to Easter,
may we spend a little time with You,
praying and giving thanks for the sacrifice
Jesus made on our behalf.

Amen.

Lenten Season 2

Almighty God,

In this Lenten season,
bring us to a place of reflection.
Help us explore, more deeply,
our place in Your plan for humanity—
just as we are, just one person chosen and loved by You,
charged to be a beacon of light, and
welcoming others to hear
the good news of Your gift of salvation.

"Come," You say, "share my message. Be a part of my pilgrimage.
I will show you the way."

Amen.

Maundy Thursday: Love One Another

Almighty God,

So many events unfolded on Maundy Thursday.
We celebrate them concluding with today: Jesus washing the disciples' feet, the first communion,
and the commission of a new commandment to
love one another as Jesus loved us.
We struggle with this commandment.
We truly do not love one another as Jesus loved us.
Sometimes we try, and sometimes we don't. We do fail and confess it to You now.
What makes us unable to fully commit to honoring this commandment?
Maybe we are worshiping the wrong things: power, money, position, and ego.
Yes, these things are present and thriving in our lives.

Deliver us, Lord, from our own undoing.

Help us keep our sights on You and the gift of Your love, which is given to us so freely and at such a high price.

A beautiful, pure love, which is nonjudgmental. We are reaching for it. As we receive it, may we remember to share it and to pass it on.

Amen.

Lenten Season Reflections

Almighty God,

In this Lenten season, we pause to reflect on the events
leading up to Jesus's crucifixion.
Great hope was dashed, all was dark,
and the earth shook. All was lost—
or so the people thought.

When Jesus rose from the dead,
a new understanding of our existence expanded before us.
No one could have ever imagined it.
Your plan was so vast, we couldn't even begin to consider it.
Does that sense of amazement remain in us?

Yes, Lord, it does, and we are so deeply grateful
for Your incredible gifts, which are Your forgiveness of our sins
and Your promise of eternal life.

You neither turned Your back
nor gave up on us. You simply said,
"Try harder. I love you, and you are not forgotten."

How humbled we are to hear these words.
Our total gratitude we offer to You.

All honor and glory be Thine,
magnificent Lord, Creator of all.

Amen.

Little Miracles All around Us

Loving God,

In this most holy season,
please open our eyes to
all of the little miracles that surround us.
We miss so much by not being observant.
Your love is at work all around us.

Awaken Your awareness in us,
that we might celebrate Your presence
with newfound understanding.

Amen.

Spring and Possibilities

Loving God,

Spring is blossoming all around us.
Gardens are radiant with
colors, shapes, and scents.
There is renewed hope
and possibility in the air.

May we breathe in that hope and possibility.
Open us to the glorious opportunities
You have placed around us.
Help us to celebrate our place
in the garden of life,
as we celebrate the joy of our existence
and our special relationship with You.

Amen.

10

Holiday Prayers

Each of our holidays has significance and a celebration, from the hopeful New Year's Day celebration through the end of year. Our most celebrated holiday is Christmas with the gift of our Lord Jesus.

Each holiday offers opportunities to explore our faith and seek inspiration to live in a more thoughtful way. Gatherings of friends and family, sharing, celebrating, and loving each other, are gifts from above.

New Year Aspirations

Heavenly Father,

As we begin the new year,
draw us close to You.
Let us feel Your presence in our lives.

Strengthen our resolve to be kinder,
more loving people. May we take time each day
to engage You in prayer and to express our gratitude
for all the blessings You have bestowed upon us.

We have so much to be thankful for.
Keep us on the right path
and help us to make choices
that reflect our love for You.

Amen.

Veteran's Day

Almighty God,

This Veterans Day, we honor all veterans, past and present,
for the sacrifices they made on our behalf.
We ask that You watch over all our
servicemen and women on active duty.

Please give comfort to those who have lost loved ones
while serving our country.
Help those who have returned from war with wounds and
injuries.
Heal, uplift, and watch over them and our country, we pray.

Amen.

Valentine's Day

Heavenly Father,

Today we celebrate Valentine's Day
with expressions of love.
Any opportunity to share love is always welcomed.

"I love you," is such a connecting sentiment.
It fills us with warmth.
It makes us feel valued.
We do love You, Lord.
We appreciate all the blessings You have given us.

There is so much to praise You for,
especially Your watching over us,
caring for us, and always being by our side.

We are your beloved children.
Thank You, Lord God, for blessing us so richly.

Amen.

Easter Week

Almighty God,

What an array of events took place
during the first Easter week.
It was a dichotomy of the human condition—
death and eternal life.

What a range of emotions were spread across that week—
celebration, jealousy, betrayal, suffering, and loss.
Then, in great despair, amidst the fear that it was all over,
the miraculous occurred.

Jesus rose from the dead.

From that time forward, we have been amazed
at how the events have unfolded.

Today, with all the struggles and despair
we still must face in our lives,
we have the hope
of a better time, a better place,
and ultimately, salvation and eternal life.

How do we express gratitude to You for gifts
so great that everything else pales in comparison?

You ask so little of us.
You ask that we spread the love
You have given us.

You ask us to be kind and thoughtful in our actions
and to remember to spend time with You.

We shall try, dear Lord,
to honor You by our actions. We shall try.

Amen.

Journey to the Cross

Ever-present God,

As we proceed solemnly toward Friday and the Crucifixion,
we reflect upon events of that day.
All was dark, and all hope seemed lost.
Sadness overwhelmed us.
We could not see the great promise
that would be fulfilled.

All was not lost after all.
We were not alone and deserted.
Great hope and fulfillment were just beyond our sight.

As Easter morning dawns,
may we, again, be filled with the joy of new life
and the promise of forgiveness.
All is new, and hope prevails.

How magnificent You are, Our Lord.
How blessed are we to be called Your children.

Amen.

Easter Day

Alleluia, alleluia!

O Father, how we sing and shout Your praises!
Sin and death were defied!
We have been given salvation and eternal life.

Alleluia!

Your love is victorious.
We are saved!

Alleluia!

Our grateful hearts are filled with praise for You, our Lord.
We lift our voices in song to You, our Redeemer.
May Your love envelop us.
May it spread to one and all.
May Your glory be carried
in our hearts and our songs.

Easter morning has dawned.

Alleluia!

Amen.

The Gifts of Easter

Loving God,

How magnificent You are—
from creation to
a promise so big that it is boundless.

Easter now has passed,
but the promise of salvation
and eternal life are here forever.
We could repeat and repeat that message,
and it would never get old.

So we stand here before You
with grateful hearts.
You have filled us with a hope
that shall never fade.
Lead us, Lord, where You wish us to go.
Keep us ever mindful of that hope,
as we live each day.

Amen.

Easter Now Has Passed

Heavenly Father,

The Easter celebration is over.
Your praises we have sung.
The gifts of forgiveness and salvation
still gleam before us.

Death has been overcome.
We bow before You, and our
humble honor we give to You.
Our hearts are filled with gratitude
that we might live eternally.

Amen.

Thanksgiving Is Approaching

Almighty God,

Thanksgiving is fast approaching, and
even in these times of struggle in our country,
there is so much to be thankful for:
We have the majesty of this beautiful country,
which we are blessed to call our home.
We live in peace
and have the freedom to move about as we choose
and to say what we wish—these are
just a few of our blessings.

Personally, we each have blessings that come to mind.
We offer these up to You silently, in this moment.

Thank You, Lord, for being present in our lives.
Thank You for placing us where You have placed us.
Let us sing Your praises.

May we all embrace the idea of being thankful
each and every day.

Amen.

Thanksgiving Day Thoughts

Loving God,

What do we think of as we prepare for Thanksgiving?
We have so many reasons to be thankful.
We live in peace and safety.
Our community is responsive to our daily needs.
We have food, shelter, and protection.

We are especially grateful for our freedoms, which allow us
to be able to worship You and to speak our minds.
You made this beautiful country,
and You have placed us in it.

We give thanks to You for
the bounty You have given us.
In the days leading up to Thanksgiving,
may we take a moment, each day,
to commune with You in celebration of
the beauty and gifts, which surround us all year long.
May we also remember that Thanksgiving
is more than just one day in November.

Amen.

Thanksgiving

Our hearts are filled with praise for You,
O glorious Father!

Thanksgiving should be every day!
You have given us so much to enjoy.
How blessed we are by all
You have given us in this beautiful country—
rich harvests and so much plenty.

As we join with our families and friends this Thanksgiving,
may we invite You to be present with us.
We honor You and offer our lives
to You in service.

Guide us where You will.

Amen.

Thanksgiving Blessings

Glorious Father,
Thanksgiving is approaching, and with it
comes a time of prayer and reflection
on the many blessings You have bestowed upon us,
personally and as a country.

We look forward to celebrating and
giving thanks with family and friends.
As we do, we remain mindful of
many families around us who are not as fortunate.
They are suffering due to job losses, financial difficulties,
illnesses, loneliness, or problems in their own families.

Give us an awareness so we might reach out to them
and share Your love with them, using
any means we have available.

We can all do this in big or little ways.
It really doesn't matter how we do it.
What does matter is that we find a way to
spread Your love.

Father, may Your presence be felt by all
during the Thanksgiving holiday.
May joy and goodwill fill our homes.
Let those we reach out to feel Your love,
and may it give them hope and encouragement.

Your love dwells in all of us.

Amen.

Hope in the Holidays

Merciful Father,

Even in the midst of this beautiful holiday season,
there is pain, hurt, and injury. We want to be happy and
celebratory as we anticipate the coming event.
Yet sometimes, it is not easy to get to that place.

This situation is no different from when
our Lord Jesus first came into the world.
There was struggle, strife, suffering, and loss of hope.

Time hasn't changed this. Often,
we lose sight of the gift our Lord Jesus gave to us.
Yet there is hope even when
we are unable to see or feel it.
It is the olive branch held out to us
when we are feeling low and lost.

This is Your promise.

We must remember that trials will pass.
What will remain is Your gift of deliverance from our travails.
Help us, Lord, to reach out for that branch.
Encourage us when we are not able to inspire ourselves.
Our faith rests in You!

Amen.

Christmas Star

Loving God,

The Christmas star, shining forth in the night and
offering hope and a great promise,
has not diminished.
We seek its glow.

We desire to follow it as the wise men
did so many years ago.
Each year, that hope wells up in our souls.

We are so thankful for the Christ child.
Like the wise men, we wish to honor Him with our gifts.
We have not gold, myrrh, or frankincense.
But we have a treasure far greater and
one more pleasing to our Lord. Yes, let's give Him
our hearts. Let's strive to honor Him by bringing
peace and love to this world.

Let our hearts radiate that luminous star's light.
Let us share the message God sealed in it.

Amen.

Christmas Morn

Almighty God,

Oh, glorious Christmas morn,
the dawn is breaking,
and the birth, so long anticipated,
has divinely arrived.

Oh, joy, the promise is fulfilled.
Through the ages to this very day,
the gift is celebrated still,
as if it was new—no, not new.

It is timeless and eternal.

We awake on Christmas morn filled with gratitude
as we celebrate and honor the birth of Jesus.
We bow heads in praise to You for sending our Redeemer.

Hope and promise fill the air. Christmas bells ring
tides of gladness as we unite in prayer.

Amen.

11

Choir Prayers

I dedicate this chapter to my San Marino Community Church choir family. We practice each week, in preparation to sing our anthems on Sunday mornings. We also practice for our annual Christmas cantata and our Easter morning celebration. In this way, we celebrate our Lord in song. We are uplifted when we sing His praises. We close our practice in prayer. These are choir-specific prayers. You may wish to share these prayers with your choir.

Back to Church

Most loving and gracious God,

Here we begin another choir year.
We are happy to be back together.
We are eager to learn new anthems
and look forward to singing Your praises.

Thank You for this past summer.
It was a time to relax and renew.
We are so grateful to be a part of this choir
and to lift up our voices to You.

May we rededicate ourselves to our choir and church.
Please watch over our congregation—
each person and family represented here this evening.

Amen.

A New Choir Year

Most loving God,

As we begin this new choir year, we are happy to be back together. We look forward to learning new anthems and singing Your praises.

We lift our voices to You with grateful hearts
and deep appreciation for Your presence in our lives.
May our anthems return some of the joy to You
that You have given to us.

Please watch over every person and family represented here this evening.
Please help our church grow and expand and bring people
from the greater community into our family of faith,
that they may know and celebrate You better and
more fully in their lives.

Amen.

Choir Prayer: The Gift of Song

Father,
How blessed we are that You have given us
the gift of song. May our voices rise
in praise to You as we celebrate
Your greatness, compassion, and love through music.

Please accept our offering of these anthems, hymns, and songs,
in deep appreciation for all the blessings
You have bestowed upon us.
We are grateful for all of the gifts
You have given us, and we will continue to sing
Your praises throughout our lives.

Amen.

New Choir Year

Loving Father,

We stand before You at
the beginning of another choir year.
We rededicate ourselves to this choir
with the hope of honoring You in song.

We are filled with praise for You
and wish to perpetuate Your glory
through anthems and hymns.
Please keep us focused on our choir responsibilities.
Please give us all a sense of purpose and resolve.
May all our efforts bring You the joy that
Your creation of music has given to us.

We thank You, Father, for this opportunity
to serve You.

Amen.

Afterword

My goal in writing this book was to present a way to connect with the Lord in short, simple prayers. Understanding that life is complex, I wanted to celebrate our Lord and lift people up. The challenges present in life can pull us down and take us away from the joy that God intended for us. I wanted to provide a way to address these challenges in prayer.

Further, I wanted to encourage people to become more proactive in turning this world into a more God-centered place, one person at a time. It is a beginning for some. It is a supplement for others.

One thing I have learned is that our Lord is delighted when we share our lives with Him. Sharing our thoughts and concerns with our Lord is welcomed and encouraged by Him. Simple prayer is a way to begin. May you experience the joy and connection of actively sharing your life in communion with our loving God.